LAND THAT I LOVE
Regions of the United States

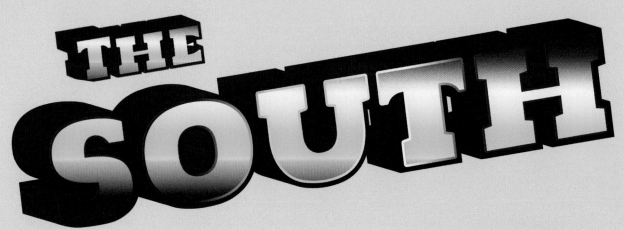

THE SOUTH

Niccole Bartley

PowerKiDS press.
New York

Published in 2015 by The Rosen Publishing Group, Inc.
29 East 21st Street, New York, NY 10010

First Edition

Editor: Joanne Randolph
Photo Research: Katie Stryker
Book Design: Colleen Bialecki

Photo Credits: Cover CBD/iStock/Thinkstock; p. 4 Pete Muller/iStock/Thinkstock; p. 5 DWalker44/iStock/Thinkstock; p. 6 Roy H. Anderson/National Geographic/Getty Images; p. 7 Hulton Archive/Handout/Getty Images; p. 8 DEA Picture Library/De Agostini/Getty Images; p. 9 John Parrot/Stocktrek Images/Getty Images; p. 10 National Archives/Handout/Hulton Archive/ Getty Images; p. 11 Joseph Scherschel/The LIFE Picture Collection/Getty Images; p. 12 Hozer/iStock/Thinkstock; p. 13 (top) Robert Kyllo/Shutterstock.com; p. 13 (bottom) vahalla/Shutterstock.com; p. 14 Dave Allen Photography/ Shutterstock.com; pp. 15, 23 (top) Jorg Hackermann/Shutterstock.com; p. 16 (top) Dean_Fikar/iStock/Shutterstock.com; p. 16 (bottom right) Jupiterimages/photos.com/Thinkstock; p. 16 (bottom left) Molly Dean/iStock/Thinkstock; p. 17 (bottom) Jupiterimages/Stockbyte/Thinkstock; p. 17 (top) Spirit of America/Shutterstock.com; p. 17 (middle) Wendell Metzen/ Photolibrary/Getty Images; p. 18 Sorbis/Shutterstock.com; p. 19 Alan Jeffery/Shutterstock.com; p. 20 Paul Brennan/ Shutterstock.com; p. 21 (top) Linda Johnsonbaugh/iStock/Thinkstock; p. 21 (bottom) Chuck Wagner/Shutterstock.com; p. 22 Andresr/Shutterstock.com; p. 23 (bottom) Henryk Sadura/Shutterstock.com; p. 24 Testa Images/Flickr/Getty Images; p. 25 (top) Jeff Greenberg/Photolibrary/Getty Images; p. 25 (bottom) Fred LaBounty/Shutterstock.com; p. 26 Natalia Bratslavsky/ Shutterstock.com; p. 27 Jaimie Duplass/Shutterstock.com; p. 28 Darryl Vest/Shutterstock.com; p. 29 JupiterImages/ Photolibrary/Getty Images; p. 30 Sean Pavone/Shutterstock.com

Library of Congress Cataloging-in-Publication Data

Bartley, Niccole.
The South / by Niccole Bartley. — First edition.
     pages cm. — (Land that I love : regions of the United States)
Includes index.
ISBN 978-1-4777-6857-0 (library binding) — ISBN 978-1-4777-6858-7 (pbk.) — ISBN 978-1-4777-6636-1 (6-pack)
1. Southern States—Juvenile literature. I. Title.
F209.3.B37 2015
975—dc23
                                   2014001271

Manufactured in the United States of America

CPSIA Compliance Information: Batch #WS14PK9: For Further Information contact Rosen Publishing, New York, New York at 1-800-237-9932

CONTENTS

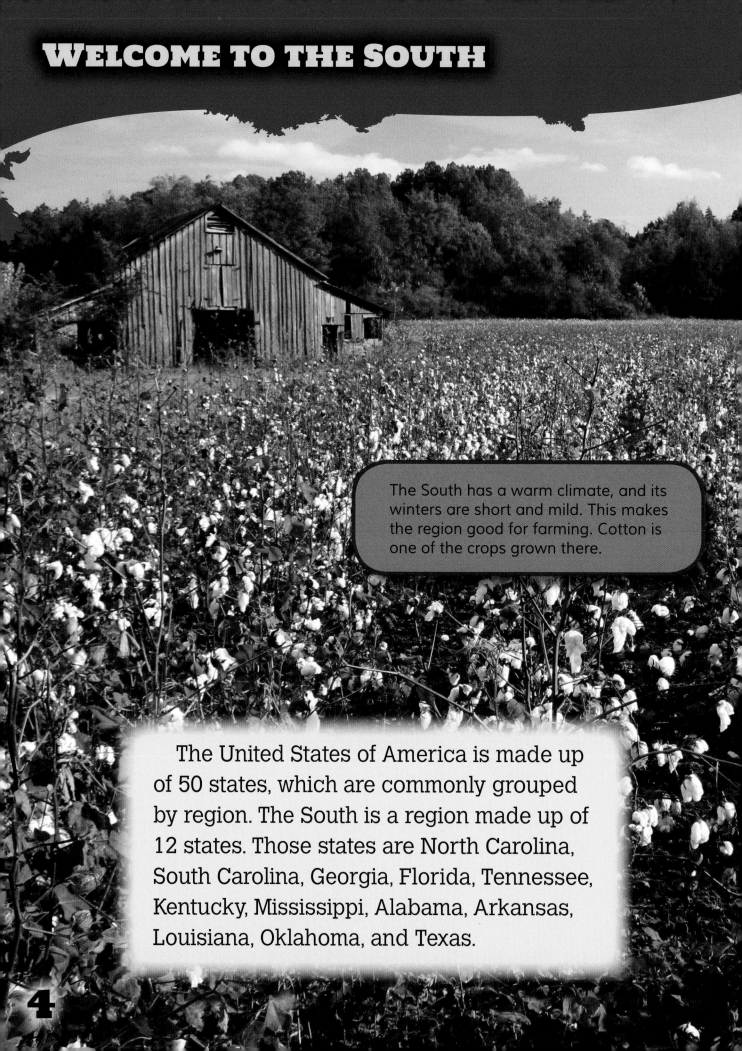

WELCOME TO THE SOUTH

The South has a warm climate, and its winters are short and mild. This makes the region good for farming. Cotton is one of the crops grown there.

The United States of America is made up of 50 states, which are commonly grouped by region. The South is a region made up of 12 states. Those states are North Carolina, South Carolina, Georgia, Florida, Tennessee, Kentucky, Mississippi, Alabama, Arkansas, Louisiana, Oklahoma, and Texas.

Savannah, Georgia, is known for its beautiful, historic homes.

The South borders the Atlantic Ocean to the east and the Gulf of Mexico to the south. The plains and prairies of Texas and Oklahoma form the western border of the South. Many southerners enjoy boating on the many lakes and rivers of the South. Some also head to the coast or mountains to escape the hot summers.

The first humans who lived in the South were called Paleo-Indians. They lived 10,000 years ago. Paleo-Indians were hunter-gatherers who roamed in bands and hunted large **mammals**.

The Paleo-Indian groups gave way to the Mississippian culture, which existed between AD 800 and AD 1500. These Native Americans made mounds and then built small villages or structures on top of the mounds.

The Paleo-Indians lived during the time of large mammals such as mastodons, mammoths, and saber-toothed tigers, which are now extinct.

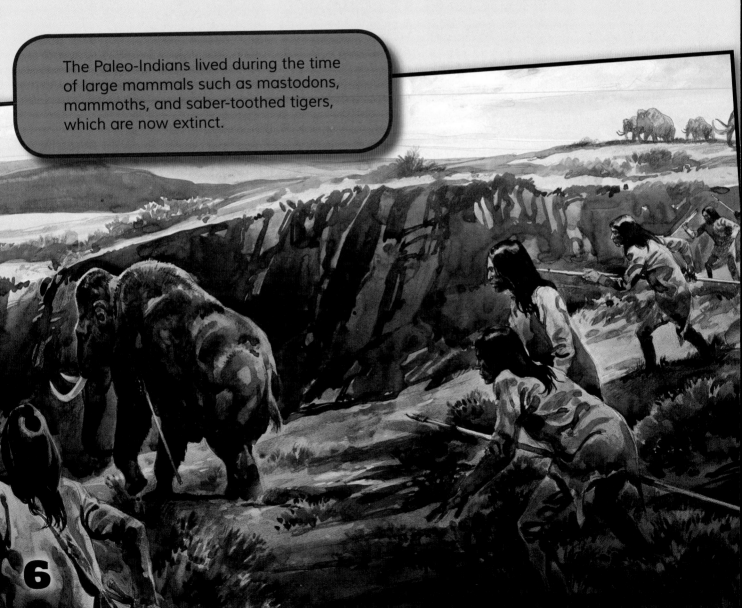

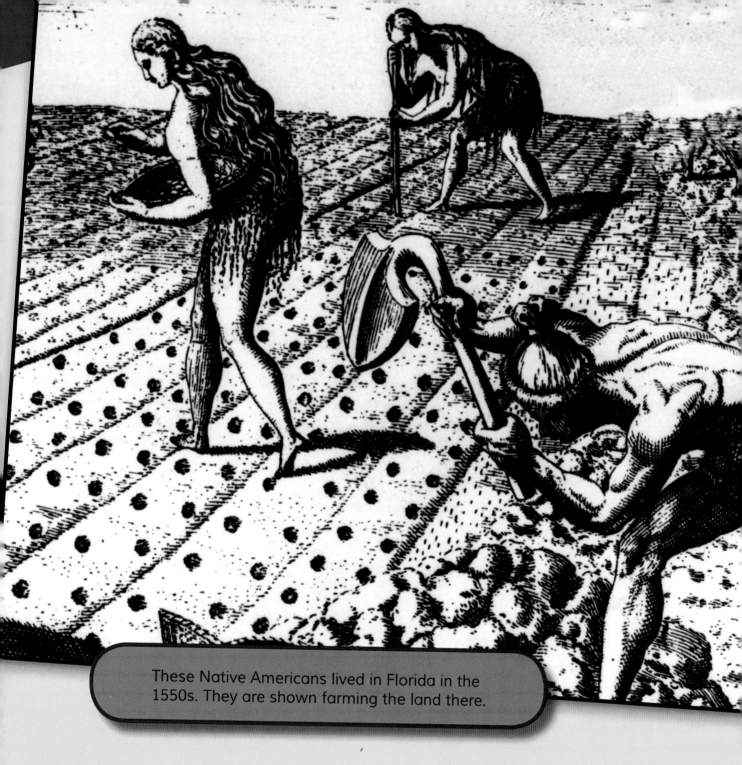

These Native Americans lived in Florida in the 1550s. They are shown farming the land there.

The mound-building society collapsed in the 1500s due to war among their people and disease brought by Europeans. The nations that lived in the South after that were **descendants** of the Mississippian peoples. Some of these tribes are the Alabama, Cherokee, Choctaw, and Seminole tribes.

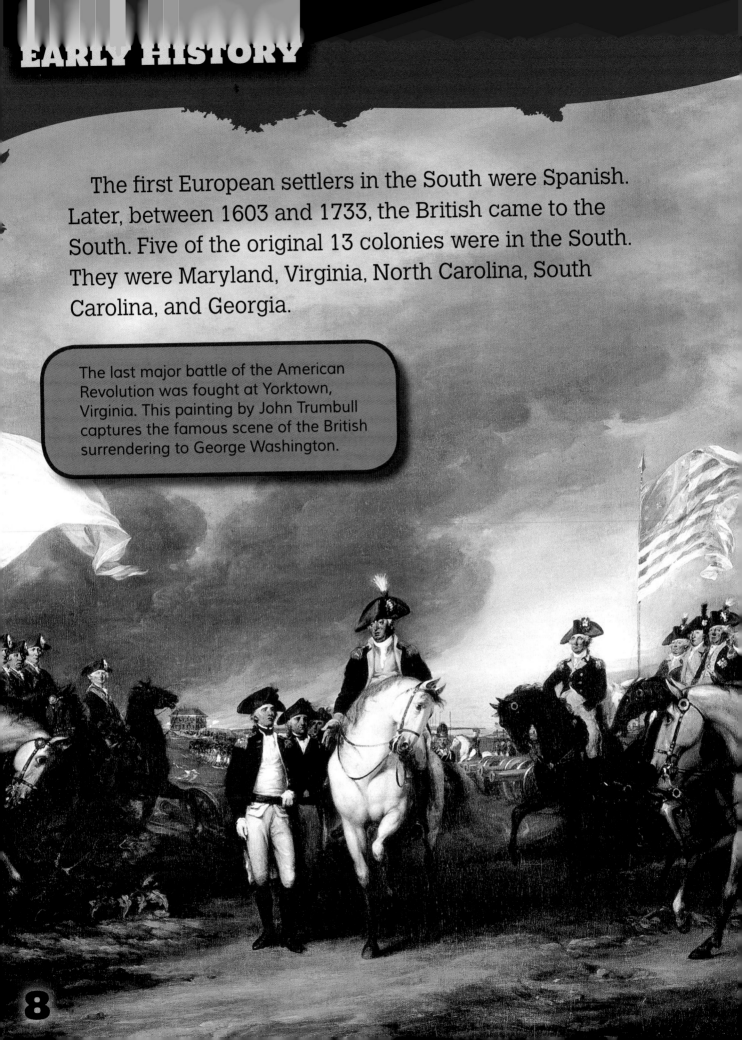

The first European settlers in the South were Spanish. Later, between 1603 and 1733, the British came to the South. Five of the original 13 colonies were in the South. They were Maryland, Virginia, North Carolina, South Carolina, and Georgia.

The last major battle of the American Revolution was fought at Yorktown, Virginia. This painting by John Trumbull captures the famous scene of the British surrendering to George Washington.

Since most of the battles of the Civil War took place in the South, including this one at Mobile Bay, Alabama, the region was destroyed. The US government spent the next decade rebuilding the South. This period is known as Reconstruction.

Since the climate in the South was mild, the South became an agricultural region. Wealthy landowners had large plantations and grew cotton and tobacco. The plantations required many workers in the fields, so the plantation owners brought slaves from Africa.

THE DUST BOWL

The Dust Bowl was a period of severe dust storms in the South and Midwest prairies from 1930 to 1936. The Dust Bowl was caused by a severe **drought** and poor farming practices. It led to a widespread disaster in farming in the Midwest and some southern states including Oklahoma and Texas. Much farmland became useless, and hundreds of thousands of people were forced to leave their homes. The loss of farmland and agricultural production worsened the **Great Depression**.

The American Revolution unified the 13 colonies in 1776. However, slavery quickly divided the nation. The Northern states thought that slavery was wrong and should be **abolished**. The Southern states believed that their way of life depended on slave labor.

In 1860, 11 Southern states left the United States to form the Confederacy. This led to the American Civil War, which lasted from 1861 to 1865. In the end, slavery was abolished and the South was defeated.

Racism against African Americans in the South persisted after the Civil War. Southern states practiced **segregation** under the **Jim Crow laws**.

These protesters are marching against segregation in schools at a civil rights rally in 1963.

The farm-based economy of the South was hit hard during the Dust Bowl. The dust storms and severe drought caused the failure of many farms, such as this one in Texas.

Segregation meant that white and black people lived, worked, and went to school in separate places. The South was segregated until the 1960s, when the **civil rights movement** led by Martin Luther King Jr. and other **activists** brought about equal rights for people of all races in the United States.

WRITE ABOUT IT!

Did you know that Texas was once its own country? It became part of the Union in 1845. Before the Civil War began, Texas decided to join the Confederacy. One of Texas's leaders, Sam Houston, strongly disagreed with this. Pretend you are Sam Houston and write a speech trying to convince the other leaders to remain in the Union.

The South is home to some of the world's most important wetlands, rivers, swamplands, and bayous. The Everglades, in Florida, is a large subtropical wetland. It is the largest wilderness area east of the Mississippi River. People visit the Everglades to enjoy many activities such as snorkeling, kayaking, camping, and wildlife boat tours.

Everglades National Park was established in 1934 and preserves 1.5 million acres (607,028 ha) of cypress and mangrove forests and saw grass marshes. People visit it to see the many species of fish, amphibians, reptiles, mammals, and birds that live in the Everglades.

The Mississippi River is used to transport goods to the ports in New Orleans to be exported overseas.

The Mississippi River is the longest river in the United States. It flows 2,530 miles (4,070 km) from Minnesota south to the Gulf of Mexico. In the 1800s, settlers moving west traveled on the Mississippi River. In the 1900s, people built many **levees** and dams to make it easier to travel and ship goods on the river.

Louisiana and parts of Texas are famous for bayous. A bayou is a very slow-moving river or bog. Bayous are home to shellfish such as crawfish and shrimp as well as catfish, frogs, and alligators.

COASTS AND MOUNTAINS

The South has a beautiful coastline and many stunning mountains. Florida has the longest coastline in the United States and borders both the Atlantic Ocean and the Gulf of Mexico.

The Great Smoky Mountains, or the Smokies, are home to more than 187,000 acres (75,676 ha) of hardwood forest and the largest black bear population in the United States.

Florida has more than 1,350 miles (2,170 km) of beaches along the Atlantic Ocean and the Gulf of Mexico. Many people who live, visit, or retire in Florida spend time at the beaches.

Five southern states border the Gulf of Mexico to the south. They are Florida, Alabama, Mississippi, Louisiana, and Texas. Many people who live there enjoy swimming, water sports, and fishing on the gulf.

There are three mountain ranges in the South. The Blue Ridge Mountains in North Carolina are known for their bluish color when seen from a distance. The Great Smoky Mountains are found in Tennessee and North Carolina. The Ozark Mountains are in Oklahoma and Arkansas.

THE SOUTH

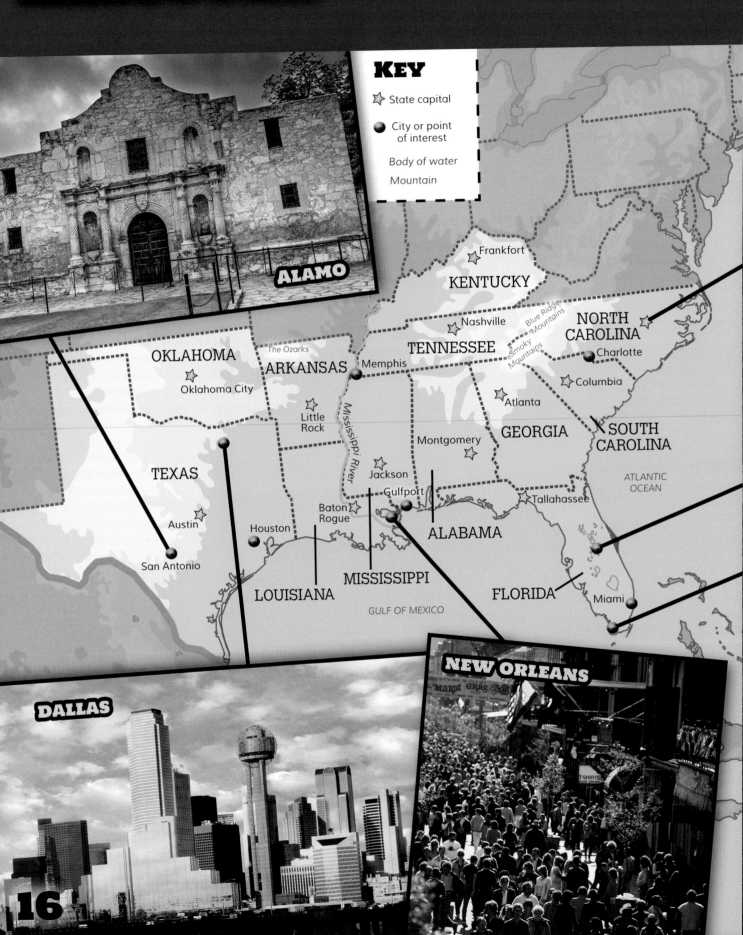

ALAMO

KEY

⭐ State capital

⬤ City or point of interest

Body of water

Mountain

Frankfort ⭐
KENTUCKY

Nashville ⭐
TENNESSEE

Blue Ridge Mountains
NORTH CAROLINA ⭐

Smoky Mountains

The Ozarks

OKLAHOMA
⭐ Oklahoma City

ARKANSAS
⬤ Memphis

Charlotte ⬤

⭐ Columbia

⭐ Atlanta

⭐ Little Rock

Mississippi River

GEORGIA

SOUTH CAROLINA

TEXAS

Montgomery ⭐

⭐ Jackson

⬤ Gulfport

ALABAMA

ATLANTIC OCEAN

⭐ Austin

⬤ Houston

Baton Rogue ⭐

⭐ Tallahassee ⬤

⬤ San Antonio

LOUISIANA

MISSISSIPPI

FLORIDA

⬤ Miami

GULF OF MEXICO

DALLAS

NEW ORLEANS

RALEIGH

DISNEY WORLD

EVERGLADES NATIONAL PARK

PLANTS AND ANIMALS OF THE REGION

The South has many unique plants and animals. Famous plants in the South are southern magnolia trees, Spanish moss, and flowering dogwoods. The Blue Ridge and Smoky Mountains have southern Appalachian spruce-fir forests, which are unlike any other forests found on Earth.

Tropical birds breed in the Florida Everglades. The Everglades are also the only place in the United States to find the Florida panther and the American crocodile. The American alligator is more common, living in swampy areas from Texas to North Carolina.

Alligators love the swampy habitats of the Everglades and bayous of the South.

The beaver is the largest rodent found in North America. It has webbed feet and a flat tail and eats plants. Beavers are nocturnal and build dams up to 20 feet (6 m) wide to create water pools, in which they can build their homes, known as lodges. An adult beaver can weigh 40 to 60 pounds (18–27 kg).

Beavers live all over the South near rivers and ponds. Early settlers and trappers almost hunted beavers to extinction for their thick fur. Today, beavers are making a comeback.

THE TEXAS LONGHORN

The Texas longhorn is a breed of cattle known for its large horns. Texas longhorns are known for their unique coloring. A longhorn can be any color or mix of colors, but dark red and white color mixes are the most common. Texas ranchers raise longhorns because they thrive in the hot, dry climate with little water in the pasture. The Texas longhorn is raised for beef.

After the Civil War, the South was very poor. Most of the large cotton and tobacco plantations were broken up into small farms. Agriculture is still a big part of the southern economy, though. Farmers in the South grow such crops as tobacco, rice, sugarcane, and citrus fruits.

In the past few decades, the South has become more **industrialized**. Since the 1960s, automobile plants have been moving to Alabama, Kentucky, Mississippi, and Tennessee. Many businesses are moving their headquarters south, too.

This field in Georgia is filled with bales of hay. Hay is used to feed livestock, such as cattle and horses.

Lumber production is a big industry in many southern states, such as Alabama and Georgia. Lumber companies cut down trees and then cut the wood into boards that can be used for building.

Commercial fishing is an important industry along the Gulf Coast, as is tourism. The discovery of oil in Texas in 1901 started an economic boom there. Texas has one-fourth of the oil reserves in the country.

Tourism is a big industry in many southern states. Thousands of tourists head to New Orleans, Louisiana, for its Mardi Gras celebration.

21

The South was very rural until the late 1940s. Today, cities in the South are growing at a fast pace. Some of the main cities of the South are Atlanta, New Orleans, Charlotte, Miami, Houston, Dallas, Memphis, Nashville, and Jackson.

Miami is home to one of the largest ports in the United States, the Port of Miami. It is the largest cruise ship port in the world. The Miami area has a big tourism industry, with many hotels and resorts in South Beach, just across Biscayne Bay from Miami.

Houston is the largest city in Texas and is home to more than six million people. It is the fourth-largest city in the country. Large petroleum companies such as Conoco-Phillips are based in Houston.

Atlanta is the capital of Georgia. Atlanta was completely burned to the ground in the Civil War. Today, Atlanta is one of the leading cities in the country. Many corporations, such as the Coca-Cola Company, Delta Air Lines, and the Home Depot, are headquartered there. Savannah is another well-known city in Georgia. It's best known for its history and beautiful homes.

New Orleans, Louisiana, and Nashville, Tennessee, are both known for their music. New Orleans is the birthplace of jazz, and Nashville is the home of the country-music industry.

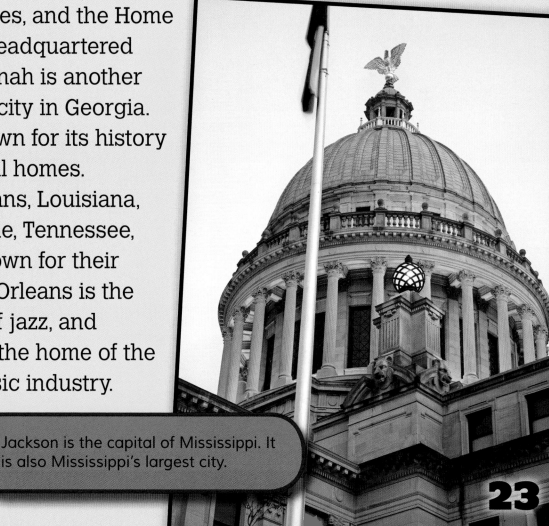

Jackson is the capital of Mississippi. It is also Mississippi's largest city.

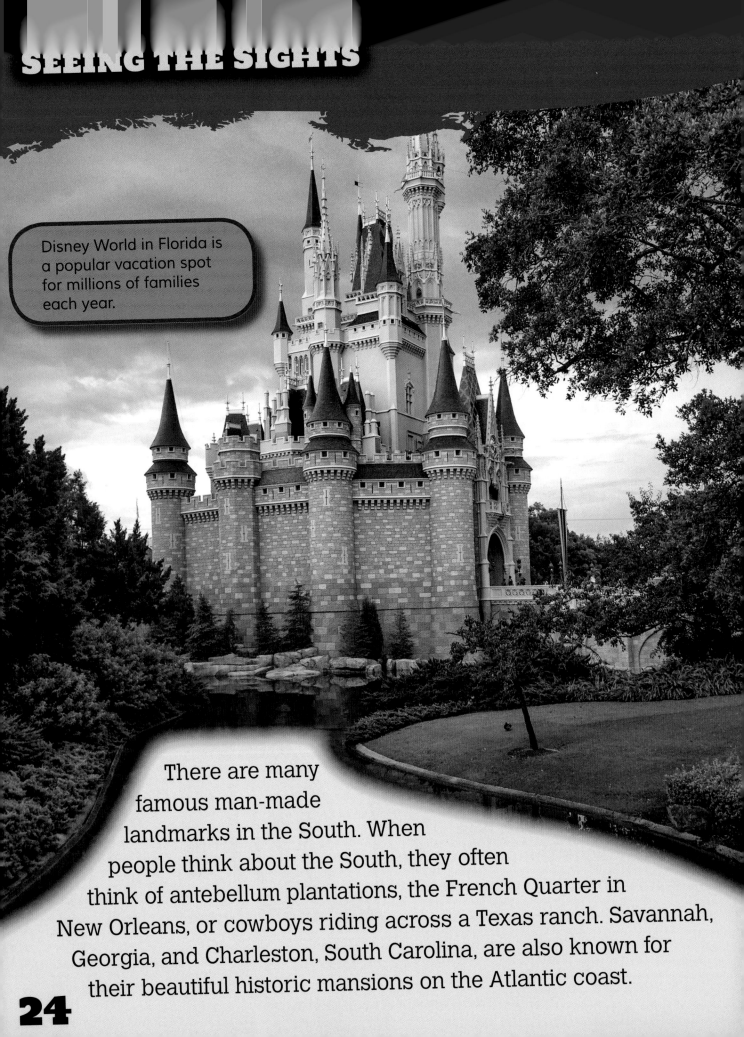

Disney World in Florida is a popular vacation spot for millions of families each year.

There are many famous man-made landmarks in the South. When people think about the South, they often think of antebellum plantations, the French Quarter in New Orleans, or cowboys riding across a Texas ranch. Savannah, Georgia, and Charleston, South Carolina, are also known for their beautiful historic mansions on the Atlantic coast.

...UNTIL JUSTICE ROLLS DOWN LIKE WATERS AND RIGHTEOUSNESS LIKE A MIGHTY STREAM

MARTIN LUTHER KING JR

The Civil Rights Memorial in Montgomery, Alabama, reminds visitors of this difficult part of our history. It has the names of 40 people who died in the fight for equal rights between 1954 and 1968.

People visiting the South often stop at Disney World in Florida, the Grand Ole Opry in Nashville, Beale Street in Memphis, and the Alamo in San Antonio. There are so many sights to see in the South.

The Alamo stands as a reminder of Texas history. The death of the defenders of the Alamo helped push the Texans to fight even harder for independence from Mexico, which they won in 1836.

The South is perhaps the most unique region in the United States. The history of the southern plantation and the legacy of slavery have shaped the culture of the South and set it apart from the rest of the country. In recent times, the South has become the most **integrated** region of the country.

Music is a big part of southern culture. Beale Street in Memphis is famous as the birthplace of rock and roll.

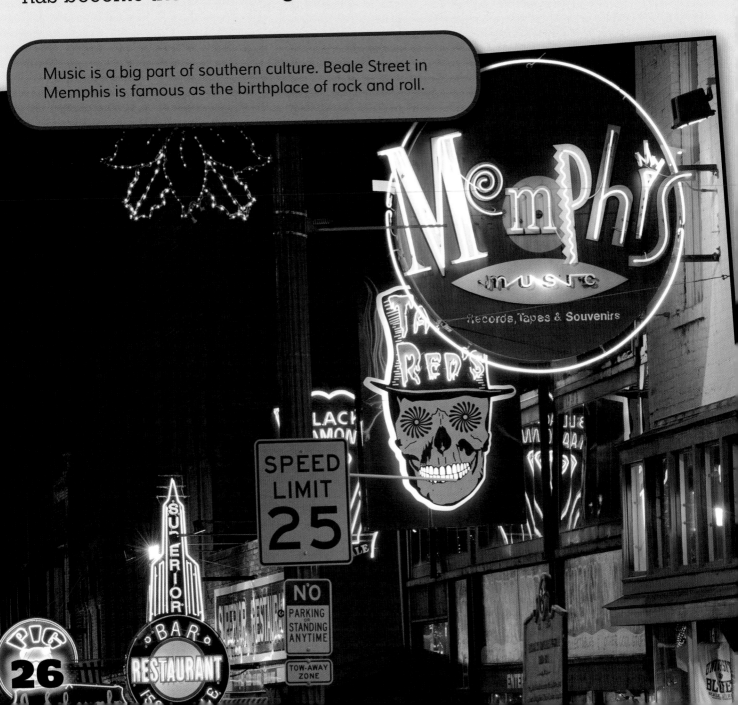

Cajun food is popular in the South, especially in Louisiana.

Southerners have their own customs, **dialects**, and music. Southern music is most celebrated in Nashville, Memphis, and New Orleans, where you can hear the sounds of jazz, blues, country, and American folk music in the places where they were born.

The most famous Southern foods are grits, fried chicken, biscuits, and barbecue. This mix of foods comes from the English settlers and the African slaves. Cajun and Creole cuisines, made famous in Louisiana, are based on French, Spanish, and other influences in the region. Tex-Mex food has influences from Mexican and Native American foods.

The South has many famous authors and its own regional literature. William Faulkner, Toni Morrison, and Margaret Mitchell are among the most famous authors. The themes of southern writing often involve slavery, plantation life, and the Civil War.

The warm waters along the coasts of many southern states and the warm weather mean that many southerners enjoy being outside and swimming, surfing, or skim boarding at the many beaches.

Many southerners come together to enjoy seafood boils. These are gatherings where the focus is generally eating shellfish or other seafood together.

REGIONAL RECIPES:
CORN SPOON BREAD

INGREDIENTS

1 cup milk
1/3 cup yellow cornmeal
1/2 teaspoon kosher salt

1 cup shredded cheddar, divided
1 cup canned corn kernels, drained
1/2 cup chopped green onions

2 large eggs, lightly beaten
2 tablespoons butter, cut in small pieces
1/8 teaspoon ground red pepper flakes

DIRECTIONS

Preheat the oven to 400° F (204° C) . In a medium saucepan, whisk together the milk, cornmeal, and salt. Cook over medium-high heat, stirring constantly, until the mixture has thickened, about 5 minutes. Stir in 1/2 cup of the cheese, the corn, and the green onion. Temper the eggs by slowly whisking some of the hot milk mixture into the beaten eggs. Stir the tempered eggs into the milk mixture. Pour the mixture into a 1-quart baking dish. Top with pieces of butter and sprinkle with the red pepper flakes and remaining 1/2 cup of cheese. Bake for 25 to 30 minutes or until the center is set and cheese is lightly browned. Remove from the oven and serve immediately.

THE NEW SOUTH

The South has a unique history. From slavery, secession from the Union, and segregation, to becoming an integrated community with a sense of place and pride, this region has come a long way. The Civil War destroyed the South, but a new South has risen from the ashes.

Southerners, black and white, have a sense of regional pride in the "New South." Today the South has evolved into a manufacturing region, and skyscrapers now dot the skylines of cities such as Houston, Atlanta, Charlotte, and Miami. The South has not lost its charm or rural character, though. The South is a special part of the United States.

Nashville, Tennessee, still holds the title of Music City, since it is the music capital of the United States. It is also home to banks, publishers, and many other businesses, too.

GLOSSARY

abolished (uh-BAH-lishd) Did away with.

activists (AK-tih-vists) People who take action for what they believe is right.

civil rights movement (SIH-vul RYTS MOOV-mint) People and groups working together to win freedom and equality for all.

descendants (dih-SEN-dents) People who are born of a certain family or group.

dialects (DY-uh-lekts) Different ways that a language is spoken in different areas.

drought (DROWT) A period of dryness that hurts crops.

Great Depression (GRAYT dih-PREH-shun) A period of American history during the late 1920s and early 1930s. Banks and businesses lost money and there were few jobs.

industrialized (in-DUS-tree-uh-lyzd) Made into a place that makes goods using power-driven machines.

integrated (IN-teh-gray-ted) Put together different parts.

Jim Crow laws (JIM KROH LOZ) Laws that were created in the late 1800s by Southern states to separate the races.

levees (LEH-veez) Raised riverbanks used to stop rivers from overflowing.

mammals (MA-mulz) Warm-blooded animals that have backbones and hair, breathe air, and feed milk to their young.

racism (RAY-sih-zum) The belief that one group or race of people, such as whites, is better than another group, such as blacks.

segregation (seh-grih-GAY-shun) The act of keeping people of one race, sex, or social class away from others.

INDEX

WEBSITES

Due to the changing nature of Internet links, PowerKids Press has developed an online list of websites related to the subject of this book. This site is updated regularly. Please use this link to access the list:

www.powerkidslinks.com/ltil/sout/